Mental Health and the Adaptation to College

A Handbook for Residence Advisors

By Philip K. McCullough, MD,
Kristen M. Granchalek, LCSW, and
Chris Ogle, MA

MENTAL HEALTH AND THE ADAPTATION TO COLLEGE
A Handbook for Residence Advisors

ISBN 978-0-692-98092-7
Philip K. McCullough M.D, S.C.

Cover design and formatting by Inventing Reality Editing Service

Manufactured in the United States of America
First printing November 2017

Acknowledgements

The authors would like to thank the following individuals for their assistance on this project:

Georganne Rojo, Editorial and IT
Karen McCullough, Editorial and IT
Patricia McCullough, Editorial and IT
Ric Damm, Ripon College, for images
The entire student services group at Ripon College
Zach Messette, President of Ripon College for support and encouragement of this project
Rob Bignell for enthusiastic editorial help

Contents

Introduction

R esearch and treatment has made clear that mental illness is caused by a combination of factors. Both biological and genetic factors are influenced by an individual's constitution, environment and history, and certain situations can trigger symptoms in the healthiest of individuals, often in response to stress or loss. The transition to college, while often positive, puts vast demands on individuals to quickly adjust to new circumstances, managing their time and behavior, all without the safety net of friends, family and close relationships. It is no wonder that the transition is bumpy for some and derailing for others.

Mental health remains a stigmatized and misunderstood issue in our society. In the wake of Newtown, Aurora, Virginia Tech, Northern Illinois University and Columbine, the imperative for early identification and intervention for mental illness is clear. Suicide is the second leading cause of death for individuals 18-34 years old. A full 75 percent of mental illness will first appear between the ages of 15-25, and students with a diagnosable mental illness have a 14 times greater risk of not completing school. Moreover, more than 40 percent of young adults in this age group report an alcohol or substance abuse issue. You need only turn on the news today to realize that the stakes for ignoring warning signs or turning away instead of toward an individual in need of assistance are too high. And while people with mental illness are more likely to be the victim of a violent crime than a perpetrator, identifying those struggling among us is imperative to the health and safety of all.

Sometimes all that stands in the way of seeking help is a lack of knowledge or simply feeling too embarrassed to speak up. Efforts to demystify mental illness and provide concrete advice to individuals in a position to refer students to treatment can make the difference between a time-limited, unsettling bump in the road and a lifelong journey toward disability and despair.

So what can we do to ensure students have access to the resources they need when they need them? This book is designed to help resident assistants and other student life professionals to differentiate between the normal "aches and pains" of adjustment to college life and the kinds of symptoms indicating the need for more serious treatment. Moreover, this book is written to provide concrete tips and advice for engaging students in delicate conversations, and to listening carefully and nonjudgmentally to gather the kinds of information you need to be of help. Our goal is to ensure that more students receive access to treatment more quickly, ensuring they get back on track without losing the kind of steam that can make completing college difficult. Our operating principle is simply this: if more individuals are armed with the kind of knowledge this book provides and can couple it with an understanding that the line between mental health and mental illness is a fine one and that all persons deserve care and compassion, people might be less afraid to speak up and take care of themselves.

This book is designed as a reference guide. **Chapter One** will provide an overview of normal development and put into context the psychological tasks that all young adults face during typical college age (18-22). It is our belief that familiarity with the "normative crises" of this age and stage will better prepare resident advisors to differentiate between the kinds of "normal stress" that can be ameliorated with support, advice and modeling, and the kinds of symptoms that indicate the need for more intensive intervention.

Chapter Two provides concrete advice and practical tips for engaging effectively with residents in an effort to generate supportive dialogue that can elicit conversation about symptoms and functioning, enabling you to intervene more effectively. Establishing empathic connection and adopting a nonjudgmental framework will provide a framework for thinking about productive engagement, intervention and triage.

Chapter 3 provides a context for understanding and assisting residents through periods of personal crisis, events that may turn otherwise developing and successful students toward instability or symptomatology. This includes death, divorce and academic difficulty, as well as other concerns.

Chapters 4-6 provide more information on the major categories of mental illness, as recognized by the current *Diagnostic and Standards Manual* issued by the American Psychological Association. We envision these chapters serving as a quick reference guide, in which you can easily identify symptoms and gain insight into a resident's possible experience. Chapters can be cross-referenced with the symptoms index in the appendix and case studies provide concrete examples of how such symptoms may present in the college population.

Chapter 7 covers other conditions affecting the adaptation to college, including learning disorders, ADD/ADHD and Autism Spectrum Disorders.

Chapter 8 addresses mental health issues specific to the LGBTQ population, where incidence of depression and suicidality are more prevalent than among heterosexual/cisgender students of the same age group. While many efforts have been made to address the ways LGBTQ youth are treated and understood in our culture, homophobia, externally experienced or internalized, continues. Supporting LGBTQ students, wherever they are along the continuum of sexuality, can improve mental health and academic outcomes for this population, as well as serve to build a culture of acceptance and openness among the wider college community.

Chapter 9 addresses issues surrounding eating disorders and body image while **Chapter 10** discusses substance abuse. **Chapter 11** speaks specifically to assisting students through the crisis of sexual assault.

Chapter 12 focuses on behaviors that may be harmful to self or others, including suicidality. This chapter will help resident assistants to identify dangerous or self-destructive behavior and intervene effectively to protect individuals and others on campus.

The book concludes with a list of national resources that can assist you in better understanding particular issues as well as resources to provide for students in need. Moreover, guidance and advice on how to identify appropriate community resources and to collaborate effectively with on campus health services are included.

We hope that this book can serve as the foundation of a broader and deeper conversation among resident assistants and across college campuses about the critical importance of supporting student mental health and emotional wellness.

Chapter 1:
Normal Development

S ince Sigmund Freud's initial theorizing about the role that unconscious process plays in the development of psychopathology, many in the field have moved toward a focus on health as opposed to illness. This philosophical shift has led professionals to study to normal psychological development to better understand the emergence of pathology. Perhaps none have made a more lasting contribution than Eric Erikson, a teacher and prolific writer, who first hypothesized about the connection between social engagement, environment and psychological development in his psychosocial development model. Erickson postulated that breaking down the lifespan into particular stages, each with associated psychological tasks, could help us to understand certain milestones and achievements that predicated healthy psychological and interpersonal development. Mastery of any one stage's challenges would continue to propel an individual toward psychological growth and maturity. The notion that earlier failures could continue to affect later development has become the basis for much of modern psychotherapy, where an important goal of long-term treatment is often to help an individual to "get back on track" developmentally by addressing the tasks to which individuals had previously failed to make successful adaptations.

Understanding normal development can have a profound effect in assisting individuals in developing empathy, for themselves and for others. Often, a coherent narrative that explains and contextualizes individual or interpersonal concerns can be immensely comforting during times of stress. It can be helpful to think of developmental theory as a framework for normalizing the aches, pains, and disappointments of everyday life as well as a tool for diagnosing when something more significant may be inhibiting a person's move toward health.

How to think about a developmental stage

During the course of a typical student's undergraduate experience, there is a transition from late adolescence to emerging adulthood. The individual arriving at college for their first year is often leaving the relative safety, security and predictability of home for the first time. The college years present a challenging time requiring personal growth and maturation. The traditional student at a residential college is in this 18-22 age group. Important transitions in the development of personality occur during these years and require a successful adaptation to changing demands. The environment of a residential college, offering a myriad of new activities, ideas and relationship, is an excellent venue for this personal growth, but it also presents significant challenges for some. By understanding this time period as the "perfect storm" of developmental change and environmental stress, it is easier to identify and understand those individuals with the natural, internal or family resources to weather such a storm better than others less well suited to the task.

Tasks of late adolescence/emerging adulthood

The characteristics of an individual's personality is not yet firmly set during late adolescence, and the college experience will be critical in shaping the course of further integration of the self. Eric Erikson defined this stage of the life cycle as a struggle to establish a sense of identify versus a feeling of role diffusion. What does this mean? Establishing a strong sense of identity is a process of trying on various roles, associating with different

Table One: Erik Erikson's Stages of Man

Approximate Age	Virtues	Psychosocial Crisis	Existential Question
Birth-1 year (Infancy)	Hope	Basic Trust vs. Mistrust	Can I Trust the World?
2-3 years (Early childhood)	Will	Autonomy vs. Shame and Doubt	Is It Okay To Be Me?
3-5 years (Pre-school)	Purpose	Initiative vs. Guilt	Is It Okay For Me To Do, Move and Act?
6-12 years (School age)	Competence	Industry vs. Inferiority	Can I Make It In The World Of People And Things?
13-25 years (Adolescence and Emerging adulthood)	Fidelity	Identity vs. Role Confusion	Who Am I? What Can I Be?
25-40 years (Young adulthood)	Love	Intimacy vs. Isolation	Can I Love?
40-65 years (Middle adulthood)	Care	Generativity vs. Stagnation	Can I Make My Life Count?
65-death (Old age)	Wisdom	Ego Integrity vs. Despair	Is It Okay To Have Been Me?

groups and individuals, and developing moral and ethical values. Clearly the residential college experience provides an excellent laboratory for these integrative processes.

But with possibility and opportunity comes risk, which can make this an unsettling period for many. The self-focus this stage inherently calls for can mean it's a lonely period of exploration for some and is often marked by generalized instability (e.g., frequent moves, all of which requiring dealing with loss). It's an age of being in between childhood and adulthood, which can lead to feelings of anxiety, inadequacy and conflict with oneself.

The ability to leave home and live independently is a key task during this period, and the resident assistant can serve as an important transitional figure in this process. Encouragement, provision of feedback, and sharing experiential observations are all potentially valuable inputs from the resident assistant. At the same time, underneath the task of identity development lies the importance of effective separation and individuation, a process that individuals are engaged in throughout life—how to develop a healthy and functional sense of interdependency. It is important to notice those students that may appear to be transitioning well to college but are overly dependent on fellow students, romantic partners, professors, staff or you as the RA for guidance or self-regulation. This may indicate a difficulty with separation and an opportunity for a psychotherapist to effectively support this individual in establishing psychological independence.

A positive undergraduate experience is associated with completing the transition from late adolescence to early adulthood. Living independently, choosing a career path, and having the capacity to maintain mature relationships are all hallmarks of a satisfactory adaptation. A healthy and successful transition from late adolescence is generally marked by a student's ability to care for him or herself in terms of the basics (e.g., hygiene, sleep, regular diet, cleanliness, and self-care), as well as the ability to develop and maintain relationships, and to function responsibly in the academic setting. Some have used the analogy of the three-legged stool—a solid leg each for work, love and play will generally result in a psychologically healthy young person. One of Sigmund Freud's earliest statements about psychological health is aptly put; it is seen in the ability for "arbeiten und leben," that is "to work and to love." Before adulthood, this can be viewed as the ability to work productively in school, and to have healthy self-love, indicated by a positive self-regard and reasonably stable self-esteem (e.g., a self-image not predicated on external validation or success).

Importance of positive adaptation

One helpful way of understanding symptoms and behavior that appears to be irrational is to think in terms of adaptation. Throughout life, individuals adapt their mental processes and interpersonal behaviors to the environment and personalities of caregivers. For example, in some families, anger is viewed as unacceptable and destructive, so from an early age, a child learns to repress anger, and it is as if the feelings no longer exist. This change is adaptive at the time, because it enables the child to feel like a cared for and valued member of the family unit. It decreases the psychological risk of rejection by caretakers. However, such adaptations, while important to early psychological survival, can eventually be maladaptive in new environments. Take the same individual, who now as a young adult, is conflict adverse and cannot articulate when he is bothered by the behavior of others. He is placed with a roommate who tends to stay up late and play loud music, and is typically inviting friends and potential love interests over at all hours of the night. While the roommate is respectful enough to ask if the individual is bothered by this behavior, our student, used to denying his emotional reactions, minimizes the stress this creates, and tacitly accepts the behavior.

He grows increasingly passive aggressive with his roommate, creating tension in the floor community, and his grades plummet because of lack of sleep and obsessive, negative thoughts about how unimportant and invisible he feels. Quickly, the situation spirals out of control, and the student decides to leave school at the end of the semester.

While this may be an extreme example, it is useful in demonstrating the epigenetic principle—that previous adaptations to developmental issues influence future development. This does not mean that students arriving at college with certain characterological patterns or tendencies are doomed. Quite the opposite. Advances in neuroscience indicate that after the in-utero period, 15-25 is the most active period of neuronal development. The college brain becomes capable of integrating information faster and more effectively. With or without intervention, the college age student's brain has the capacity for improved socioemotional processing and emotional regulation during this period, and the internal reward system is maturing. This is a moment in which students can learn to better understand themselves, what motivates them, and what feels good. All of these indicators point to this as a rich opportunity to assist students in making positive adaptations to developmental and environmental stress, all of which will contribute to exponential, iterative growth in the future.

Most undergraduates who have a successful college experiences quickly learn that the key to adapting well is time management. There are 168 hours in the week, which allows plenty of time for sleep, study, work and socialization. A typical breakdown might look like this:

- Sleep: 56 hours (8 per night)
- Class: 16 hours (typical full load)
- Class prep: 32 hours (2 per contact hour)
- Meals: 15 hours

- Personal: 10 hours (workouts, haircuts, etc.)
- Paid work or community service: 10 hours
- Free time: 33 hours!

Even with adequate sleep and plenty of time devoted to academics, there is ample extra time available for fun, additional work, or recreation. A residence assistant often can quickly spot a student who is floundering because of spending time watching excessive TV, playing video games, or surfing the net.

The Resident Assistant's role in fostering healthy development

Adjustment disorders, as well as more serious mental health issues, often have their onset during this age period. The first signs of these problems may be evident in a struggle to make a positive adjustment to this phase of development. A resident assistant can be alert to an individual student's difficulties in making a positive adaptation, as well as suggest changes that can help a student get back on course. At the same time, resident assistants need to remember that they, too, are making the necessary adjustments to young adulthood, and have neither the time, energy or training to effectively intervene in all cases. In the following chapter, we'll take a closer look at how to engage students in dialogue about their experiences, in order to more effectively refer students to appropriate supports.

Chapter 2:
Engagement

Being a resident assistant can be a tough, demanding and rewarding experience. You are asked to wear many hats, and perhaps most importantly, to demonstrate with your whole self what it means to make a successful adaptation to college. This doesn't mean that you have to be infallible or have all the answers. Quite the contrary. As a peer, your ability to demonstrate by example the ways in which you continue to tackle challenges, navigate obstacles, and further develop your skills and sense of self provide hope for your residents and classmates alike.

Being a role model extends to the ways in which you engage students to think about and take care of themselves. When introspection and self-care come naturally, negotiating the developmental changes described in Chapter One, while difficult, leads to increased self-confidence and competence. Your ability to coach, mentor and guide others through this terrain, now that you have a roadmap to do so, can provide others with the framework they need to work constructively through this and future transitions.

At the same time, it is important to remember that you are not a professional counselor or in a position to offer residents 24/7 access and support. You have your own developmental and educational goals to worry about, and your ability to effectively balance your own needs, priorities and schedules will set a positive example of how to set healthy boundaries and build healthy interdependency. Moreover, knowing oneself and one's limits is an important sign of mental wellness. It is important to remember that you too, need and deserve constructive, attentive support, whether from friends, family, your supervisor, or your own therapist.

But short of providing ongoing support, there is much a resident assistant can do to assist students in making a successful adaptation to college and to intervene effectively in cases where more intensive support may be indicated. In addition to being a positive role model, as a resident assistant you are uniquely positioned to assist students in developing a major component of mental wellness – a sense of belonging. No doubt one of your primary job duties is to foster connections among residents and to help students integrate effectively with the rest of the campus community. While reducing attrition is certainly a major goal of such early community building efforts, it is important to remember that this alone can help an otherwise struggling student to feel (perhaps for the first time), that they are part of something bigger than him or herself. Find ways to get to know your residents as individuals, and capitalize on their strengths and special interests in order to foster respect and connection.

Related to this, resident assistants can play an important role in encouraging introspection, self-awareness and accountability. Another hallmark of mental wellness is mastery, a deep sense of confidence and competence in one's ability to complete certain tasks effectively. For many, a sense of mastery is instilled early on, but for others, mastery and associated self-esteem may remain linked to external events or the approval of others. When as an RA, you take special interest in someone's authentic strengths (as opposed to trite celebrations of everyday accomplishments), you help him to know herself better and to build authentic, sustainable self-esteem. You can encourage him to keep trying when things get tough, and demonstrate that you believe in his ability to get through whatever task or project is at hand. Over time, as your relationship develops, such *realistic* confidence will come to be internalized by the student.

Engaging students in productive conversations about what's happening in their life or their internal world is a delicate but important task. Perhaps you've always been good at getting people to open up to you about their problems, but there are ways to consciously work to augment these natural abilities. Rather than thinking in terms of technique or strategy, we present the following in terms of defining the elements of a *supportive stance* you can adopt when working with residents. Elements of a strong, supportive stance all contribute to your ability to effectively role model self-awareness and healthy adaptation. These elements include: fostering relationships; using a strengths-based perspective; displaying empathy; conveying a nonjudgmental attitude; and demonstrating reliability and accountability.

Fostering relationships

The most important component of effective engagement is the relationship you have with your resident—a sense of rapport that builds trust and supports open dialogue. In fact, studies have shown that in therapy, the strength of the relationship between client and therapist accounts for far more in terms of positive outcomes than any specific technique that the therapist employs.

There are many ways to effectively develop relationships with your residents, including displaying an accessible, open manner and genuine curiosity about residents as individuals. Using open-ended questions and avoiding questions that start with "why" (which may sound unnecessarily critical or accusatory), can help engage residents in conversation, about themselves or any topic. In fact, the more you can do to build relationships and connections with residents before you have concerns or need to intervene, the stronger your impact is likely to be.

All this said, the most important thing to remember when

building relationships is that authenticity is a critical component to building trust. The old expression, "Fake it until you make it," doesn't fly in relationship-building. There will certainly be residents that you favor and those that make your skin crawl. There will be students who you are happy to support and others who feel like a consistent drain. Being authentic doesn't mean you share these feelings with your residents, but it does mean you learn to acknowledge and understand them in yourself. When you are aware of your reactions, you can hopefully work to control them, and engage students in spite of them. Your authentic acceptance of and commitment to them as individuals will be communicated by your words and actions, which will do far more to build a helping relationship than an artificially sunny disposition.

Utilizing a strengths-based perspective

Much has been written of late lamenting the "self-esteem movement" in education and parenting, and the corresponding increase in narcissism and entitlement in rising generations. No doubt you are tired of hearing your peer group maligned for these characteristics. Unfortunately, it is likely that there are more and less useful ways to help children build authentic self esteem. Constant celebration of everyday accomplishments or attempts to protect children from ever experiencing disappointment does not bode well for an individual's ability to develop a realistic view of their own strengths and weaknesses—the kind of authentic sense of self upon which mental wellness is based.

Utilizing a strengths-based perspective does not mean approaching every resident as a "winner" or finding ways to recognize all contributions equally. Rather, a strengths-based perspective means working hard (and in some cases it may be hard!) to recognize what is *healthy, resilient* and *capable* in each of your residents, despite any obvious difficulties. A helpful exercise could be to sit down and write something concrete that you can recognize as positive—healthy, resilient, or capable—about each of your residents. Then make this list something you draw upon or refer to when thinking about how to engage or interact with a student. These ideas can become the building blocks to help a struggling student build upon their own internal resources. Finally, a strengths-based perspective means embracing a seemingly paradoxical perspective—"This person is doing their best to adapt right now...AND...This person can do better." Such a perspective helps foster authenticity, and assists residents in building self-awareness and accountability.

Displaying empathy

In psychotherapy, empathy is generally seen as one of the most important tools we have to understand, engage and effectively intervene with clients. Unlike sympathy—feeling pity or sorrow for someone's misfortunes—empathy requires you to stand in the shoes of another, and to understand and *share* the feelings they are experiencing.

This can be a tall order, and requires years of training and experience to master in a way that helps the client heal yet not overwhelm the therapist. However, we note it here because of the importance of considering the concerns and problems of residents from their perspective. Depending on history, circumstance, personality and any number of contributing factors, what may be a minor hiccup for one resident may feel catastrophic to another. What may seem like small potatoes to you may seem like an unmanageable crisis to the guy down the hall. Most importantly, the issue you navigated successfully last semester—a failing grade on a paper, your parents' divorce, a break up—may be nothing like what the student in front of you is facing, despite superficially similar circumstances.

To the extent you are able, try to listen to your resident's concerns from their perspective, and don't be too quick to jump in to commiserate about your own situation, or to provide advice or solutions. Often, the simple act of listening and validating the students' feelings and experience can be enough to bolster their confidence in their own ability to forge a constructive path ahead. Let them be the one to ask about your own experience with similar circumstances, or to solicit advice on working through a particular challenge. And keep in mind, when it's really hard to empathize or understand where a student is coming from, it can be an important indicator that they could benefit from professional help.

Conveying a nonjudgmental stance

Related to empathy, conveying a nonjudgmental stance means privileging your resident's position before jumping in with your own thoughts, feelings and advice. It means remembering that your background—gender, sexuality, race, class, and development—all influence your perspective in ways of which you may not even be aware.

What's more important to remember is that a nonjudgmental attitude will be communicated before you even have an opportunity to engage residents in one-on-one conversation by the way you decorate your room or the hall, the kinds of language you use in meetings, and the variety of activities you plan. You set the tone for what is "normal," and as is often said, with great power comes great responsibility. Finds ways to create safe, open opportunities for dialogue, and speak openly with residents about just how "normal" it is to be experiencing the stress and strain that comes with the transition to college. Demonstrate that you welcome conversations about difficult topics and that you accept students where they are: without judgment.

Demonstrating reliability and accountability

As a role model and supportive person, being reliable and

Table 2: Signals of student distress

Excessive procrastination	Threats regarding self or others
Decrease in the quality of work	Marked changes in behavior
Too frequent visits	Flat affect (failure to show emotions)
Listlessness, reports of sleeping through class	Under-responding to academic notice
Crying	Lack of follow-through
Incongruous affect (smiling while crying)	Unable to describe own emotions
Marked changes in hygiene	Chronically skipping class

accountable will take you far, not only in engaging residents, but in helping them to help themselves. When a resident is feeling lonely, helpless or insignificant, ensuring active follow-up demonstrates that you take them seriously and that their concerns are important to you. Rather than assign "homework," work together with a struggling student to co-create a concrete plan of action—specific tasks that will help him or her make more adaptive choices. This kind of collaborative problem solving can assist students in taking ownership of their own success.

And while you should always follow up with students after a discussion or problem-solving session, also encourage them to reach out to others to ensure further support and accountability. Encourage them to tell friends, family or professors about their goals and plan of action (e.g., getting up for breakfast every morning, or only going out on weekends), to rally encouragement. Demonstrate that there is no shame in reaching out for support, and frame the exercise as an experiment—one designed to learn about the self and try new skills that will hopefully be both adaptive and beneficial.

As a resident assistant, the amount of contact you have with residents on an ongoing basis means you are in a position to notice when students may be experiencing significant stress or something even more challenging. The remainder of this book will provide you with additional details to help you and your resident address specific concerns, but in general, there are a number of "warning signs" that indicate a student may require more serious intervention.

Chapter 3:
Personal Crisis

Steven is the youngest of four brothers, and the last of his siblings to leave the nest. He manages the transition well, making friends easily, walking on to the basketball team, and getting more interested in his political science major. During his first year in college, he receives word that his parents have decided to divorce, and the news throws Steven into a tailspin. He has a difficult time sleeping and work starts to pile up. He approaches you for help in a panic, when he isn't sure he can complete a major research paper on time.

Steven is experiencing a personal crisis.

Stress and crisis are words commonly thrown around by many students these days to describe their reactions to the day-to-day vicissitudes of life. However, from a clinical perspective, crisis is used to describe a moment in which an experience of stress or circumstance overwhelms an individual's usual coping mechanisms such that they cannot reasonably adapt or adjust to the change. Parental divorce, death, a break up, personal injury, and academic failure are all examples of personal crises a typical college student may face.

Crisis can be experienced due to external events, as described in the case of Steven, or internal responses to stress, e.g., the separation anxiety caused by the transition to college. Developmental challenges, like the transition to young adulthood, can themselves create a state of crisis for certain individuals, whose individual coping strategies may be overly rigid or limited.

The important thing to remember about a personal crisis is that it is indeed, personal. What is a stressful period for one student may feel apocalyptic to another. Addressing a student where he or she is can be critical to facilitating the kind of helpful dialogue that can help a student get back on course. Listen for evidence of breakdown in coping: difficulty sleeping, eating, or maintaining interest in typical activities are reasonable indicators of a problem. Many students may be resistant to acknowledge the link between stressful events and their changed mood. Some may not be aware of the connection. By gently normalizing the response they are having, you can help create room for constructive intervention.

Short-term therapy often can be quite ameliorative in addressing personal crisis. Advice, support and direction, as well as assisting the student in regaining a sense of mastery and autonomy are very effective interventions. Moreover, if an individual can effectively resolve a personal crisis, he or she may find new strength and resiliency, and will be able to move forward with a sense of meaning and renewed agency and control. These can be important messages to communicate when attempting to refer a student to a therapist or counselor.

Without proper support and intervention, a personal crisis may become the precipitant for a more serious mental health issue, like a major depressive episode. For example, a bad breakup may lead to an expectable period of grieving, but perhaps the person internalizes the breakup as proof of their undesirability. Without support, the blow to their self-esteem, accompanied by the disruption in their social life, may cause the individual to become increasingly isolated and spiral into a serious depression. Early, supportive intervention may have been able to interrupt this cycle before such destructive thoughts were able to take hold. This illustrates the importance of early identification and active support during periods of emotional upheaval.

If a resident confides in you about a personal crisis, listen with an open mind, and help them to discuss what the crisis means to them. Try to avoid attempts to minimize the individual's feelings or to persuade them that it isn't that big of a deal. Often, the process of sharing one's feelings and concerns can itself be helpful to an individual. Listen carefully for disordered thinking, which will help you decide whether a therapy or counseling referral would be indicated. Expressions of guilt, hopelessness or responsibility, for example, should be taken seriously, as they could indicate the crisis is triggering a depressive episode. Whether a referral is made or not, remember to check in with the student periodically to see how they are doing. Let them know that you remain open to hearing about their concerns, and that you're committed to helping them through.

Chapter 4:
Anxiety Disorders

Anxiety disorders are the most common mental health problems seen in adults. More than 17 percent of the adult population suffers from one of the anxiety disorders. Anxiety disorder is diagnosed nearly twice as often in women. The anxiety disorders differ from normal worry in terms of intensity and frequency as well as the significant disability that often results.

Anxiety is an unpleasant, diffuse sense of apprehension often accompanied by physical symptoms such as headaches, heart palpitations, an upset stomach, and restlessness. It is physiologically similar to fear, which is a response to a definite external threat.

Symptoms of anxiety may be caused or exacerbated by a variety of medical conditions, as well as induced by a variety of substances, most typically caffeine. Many of the anxiety disorders first present in late adolescence or early adulthood, so the typical college age population is often affected.

Anxiety may affect a student's ability to interact with others as well as limit attendance at class. Courses that require class discussion and presentations may be especially difficult for the student with an anxiety disorder. Referral to student health or counseling services for an evaluation is important as these disorders tend to respond well to treatment. Students with anxiety disorders may attempt to medicate themselves with alcohol or marijuana in an attempt to control their symptoms, but this approach often can inadvertently increase symptomatology. Below is a brief synopsis of the major categories of anxiety disorders.

Panic Disorder

Jim, a first-year student, had been making a reasonably good adjustment to school. He was popular on his floor in the dorm and had started to participate in student government. One day in the large reading room of the library, while cramming for finals and having finished yet another Starbucks, he began to feel lightheaded. Jim's pulse began to race, and he felt that his heart was going to jump out of his chest. He felt an urgent need to flee and went to the restroom to throw cold water on his face.

Jim was experiencing his first panic attack.

Panic attacks are characterized by the acute onset of intense fear. The afflicted individual often feels that they are dying or going crazy. Attacks generally last for a few minutes, but the intensity of the symptoms often causes the individual to call 911 or go to the hospital ER.

Panic disorder often presents for the first time during the college years. If untreated, panic disorder may lead to agoraphobia. You may be more familiar with this term as descriptive of someone afraid to or unwilling to leave their house (in Greek, it translates to "fear of the marketplace"), but technically, agoraphobia refers to the intense fear of having another panic attack, which leads to symptoms of avoidance of certain spaces. Stores, crowds and large lecture halls are common spots that are avoided, and it is important to intervene before avoidance patterns ossify. From 2 to 3 percent of the population have panic disorder. Treatment generally involves medication and/or psychotherapy.

Obsessive-Compusive Disorder

Jack was a conscientious and hardworking first-year student. His residence was extremely tidy and orderly, and he often spent time cleaning his room. During the middle of the first semester, you notice him having some apparent difficulty entering and exiting his dorm room, specifically a habit of checking and rechecking that the door is locked.

Jack is showing signs and symptoms of obsessive-compulsive disorder (OCD).

This disorder is characterized by the presence of obsessive thoughts and/or compulsive behaviors. Obsessions are intrusive thoughts such as fears of contamination, a need for symmetry, or aggressive or sexual impulses. They are considered senseless or threatening, but the individual has difficulty suppressing them. Compulsions are repetitive behaviors that tend to be performed in a ritualistic fashion. Compulsions include hand-washing, checking, counting, and hoarding. Often, the compulsions demonstrate a kind of "magical thinking," as the student may undertake the behavior in an effort to ward off or "undo" the obsessive thoughts (e.g., obsessive thoughts about contamination are warded off by compulsive handwashing).

OCD symptoms often wax and wane but tend to be chronic and recurrent, particularly during times of high stress. Approximately 2 to 3 percent of the population is affected with males and females equally represented. Age of onset is generally prior to age 25. OCD is treated with medication and/or behavioral therapy.

Post-Traumatic Stress Disorder

Rachel is starting school as a first-year student and is a resident on your dorm floor. She is a bit quiet and detached and keeps to herself. You have noticed she avoids attending many social events. Rachel's roommate reports she often awakens in the middle of the night in distress from nightmares. In discussing her apparent discomfort, Rachel reports to you that she was the victim of a sexual assault in the summer following her high school graduation.

Rachel is showing signs and symptoms of post-traumatic stress disorder.

PTSD is an anxiety disorder triggered by a traumatic event, which precedes the onset of symptoms. Common triggering events are sexual assault, accidents and other criminal victimizations. Service personnel returning to school after combat experiences are at high risk for PTSD. At some point following the antecedent trauma, symptoms begin to develop. Normally individuals will experience an emotional response to the specific trauma, characterized by acute numbing. Individuals will re-experience the event in different ways, such as flashbacks, intrusive thoughts and nightmares. There is a persistent avoidance of stimuli associated with the trauma and a general psychic numbing. Finally, there is evidence of arousal of the autonomic nervous system with irritability, hypervigilance, and sleep difficulty. There is growing evidence that early intervention after a traumatic event may decrease the incidence and severity of PTSD symptoms. Both medication and psychosocial treatments may be effective. PTSD can occur at any age.

Generalized Anxiety Disorder

Susan, a first-year student in your residence hall, often feels physically ill. Her stomach is often upset, causing her to miss meals in the dining hall. She often has severe head and neck aches and frequently feels "wiped out." Multiple trips to the student health service did not result in any clear diagnosis or definitive treatment. Susan was a "worrier" and frequently seemed pre-occupied.

Susan is dealing with generalized anxiety disorder.

GAD is characterized by chronic worry, nervousness, or apprehension. Physical symptoms are commonly present and include fatigue, muscle tension, headache, and a variety of gastrointestinal symptoms. Prevalence is approximately 5 percent, and the disorder is diagnosed twice as often in women.

Stress may cause a worsening of symptoms. Individuals with GAD tend to utilize medical services at an increased rate compared to their peers. Effective treatment includes both counseling and medications.

Social Anxiety

Steve is a first-year student on your floor in his second semester. He appeared to adjust well to college in his first semester and achieved recognition on the dean's list with excellent grades. On the floor, he seemed a bit quiet and shy. Steve sought you out upon return from his first class in a public speaking course. He is very distressed to find that the class required each student to present several talks. Steve wants to drop the class.

Steve is dealing with social anxiety.

Social anxiety disorder, also known as social phobia, can be a very chronic and disabling condition. This disorder is characterized by intense fear of certain situations that could be embarrassing or humiliating. This disorder is the most common of the anxiety disorders with a lifetime prevalence of 13 percent. It is slightly more common in women. Common situations that trigger anxiety and/or cause avoidance are meeting new people, speaking with authority figures, dating, going to a party or social event, speaking or performing in public and using public restrooms. Clearly problems in these situations can cause extreme difficulties for the college student in terms of academics and social interactions.

Some individuals have a non-generalized form of social anxiety, which is limited to specific situations such as public speaking. Most individuals have a generalized form of social anxiety with multiple situations triggering symptomatic responses.

Referral for treatment with medication and/or therapy can be extremely useful in controlling symptoms and limiting dysfunction and disability.

Summary

Since anxiety disorders are extremely common, often have an age of onset in the college age group, and can be extremely disruptive both in terms of academic performance and social and interpersonal relations, early identification and referral can make a tremendous difference for the student. An observant resident assistant can suggest an evaluation at student health or the student-counseling center or provide a referral to an individual therapist in the community.

Chapter 5:
Mood Disorders

*F*rank, *a first-year student, appeared to be making a fine adjustment to college. Frank made A's and B's on his midterms and was active socially and with intramurals. In early November, however, he began to feel tired and sluggish. Frank started to miss early morning classes because he could not wake up in time. He began to crave sweets and gained several pounds in a matter of a few weeks.*

Frank was suffering from an episode of major depression with a seasonal component.

Mood disorders are extraordinarily common, with a lifetime risk of one in four women and one in six males. The onset of a mood disorder during the college years is quite common.

Major Depression

Symptoms of depression present with feelings of sadness or irritability. Often sleep disturbance, fatigue and a diffuse variety of physical complaints accompany these emotional and cognitive changes.

Sometimes it can be difficult to distinguish between a "bad mood" and a depressive episode, which can lead to minimization of symptoms. "I'm just in a funk," is a common retort to expressions of concern. Time is helpful here. To qualify as a depressive episode, systems should be present for at least two weeks. Alternatively, if students have a history of depression (a reasonable inquiry if your suspicions are aroused), chances are high they are experiencing a recurrence.

The presence of at least five of the following symptoms over a two-week period implies the presence of a major depressive episode:

1. Depressed mood: Feeling sad or tearful
2. Decreased interest in activities or the inability to enjoy them
3. Significant change in weight or appetite
4. Sleep disturbance: too much or too little
5. Psychomotor agitation or retardation
6. Fatigue or loss of energy
7. Feelings of worthlessness, excessive or inappropriate guilt
8. Diminished concentration, indecision
9. Thoughts of death or self-harm (For more on managing suicidal behavior or ideation, please see Chapter 12.)

Depressive symptoms in college students often lead to academic difficulties—falling grades, poor attendance, and incompletes. Poor academic performance then adds to diminished self-esteem and anxiety regarding classroom performance, and a shameful and unnecessary spiral can ensue. Fortunately, depression is very treatable and is responsive to medication, psychotherapy and/or a combination of the two. A timely referral for evaluation can make all the difference.

Bipolar Disorder

Max, a first-year student on your floor, is a popular and active student, often initiating spontaneous social activities. During the middle of the semester, you notice that Max is often "pulling all-nighters." His speech is rapid, and he seems to be euphoric.

Max is experiencing his first episode of bipolar Disorder.

Bipolar disorder is characterized by cyclical changes in mood, alternating between depression and mania. Approximately 1.5 percent of the adult population is diagnosed. The sexes are equally represented, and the typical age of onset is late-teens to early adulthood. Bipolar disorder is a chronic, life long illness.

Manic patients present with elevated mood, pressured speech, impulsive and at times dangerous behavior, and very poor judgment. Irritability is also common. Excessive physical activity, exorbitant spending, inappropriate generosity, or indiscriminate sexual activity also can be indicators of a manic episode. Individuals often do not realize they are ill and may be resistant to treatment interventions. It also can be difficult in the early stages to differentiate between someone who's the "life of the party" and someone whose life is growing increasingly out of control. There can be a frenetic quality to the student's fun, a compulsive, driven way of behaving or communicating, that elicit an uncomfortable or distancing reaction from those closest to them. Listen careful for resident concerns.

Individuals having a manic episode require an urgent psychiatric consultation and medication, and in some cases, may require hospitalization to ensure stabilization. Adherence to a regime of maintenance medication and long-term supportive therapy can often prevent future episodes of illness.

Chapter 6:
Psychotic Disorders

J ames is a quiet and somewhat shy first-year student on your residence floor. Mid-way through the first semester, you have heard from several students that James has been wandering around the halls late at night, appearing to be pre-occupied and very much to himself. Subsequently, you learn James has been missing quite a few classes. When you approach him to "check in" with him, he seems very distracted and unable to focus. His responses are slow and tangential.

James is suffering from a psychotic disorder.

The hallmark of psychosis is a disordered thought processes. Thinking tends to be disrupted and disorganized. Often thoughts are distorted and illogical. Individuals with psychotic disorders have problems with reality testing, in other words, differentiating what is real versus fantasy or imagination is impaired.

There are a number of specific symptoms of disordered thinking associated with psychosis. Delusions are fixed, false beliefs based on highly illogical misinterpretations of events or experiences. Examples of common delusions include: a belief that one's thoughts or actions are controlled by outside forces; a belief that one has extraordinary powers; a belief that remarks of others have a special meaning; and feeling that one's thoughts can be transmitted telepathically.

Hallucinations typically occur during an episode of psychosis. Hallucinations are disorders of perception and may involve any of the senses. Most commonly, individuals experience auditory hallucinations, usually in the form of voices commenting on the individual's activities. The voices are often mean, critical and degrading. Command hallucinations may order the individual to perform harmful acts.

Disorganized speech and behaviors are symptomatic of psychosis. Individuals may create new words (neologisms), experience thought blocking resulting in an abrupt halt in speaking, and may be incoherent when attempting to express themselves. Unusual behaviors seem in psychosis include posturing, inappropriate social behaviors or laughter, neglect of hygiene, or bizarre clothing and appearance.

Psychosis may have many causes. Some are related to general medical conditions or toxicity due to drugs. Schizophrenia and related disorders (schizophreniform, schizoaffective and brief reactive psychosis) present with psychotic symptoms and first break disorders often are seen in the college age group. Bipolar manic patients may present with psychotic symptoms.

Psychosis is an emergency situation and requires immediate medical and psychiatric evaluation and treatment. Once the proper diagnosis is made, medications can be effective in minutes or hours.

It is important to remember that for many individuals experiencing a psychotic episode, they are terrified and anxious. While witnessing such behavior can be alarming and upsetting for you or other residents, it is likely the individual suffering is very scared and feels out of control. To find empathy, it can be helpful to understand that psychotic individuals have a hard time differentiating inside from outside, internal from external. Such sensations can make it hard to feel separate, distinct and safe from those around you.

Try to remain calm and to be compassionate. Do your best to keep the individual calm and comfortable as you arrange for a psychiatric or medical evaluation, and request support if you don't feel safe being alone with the student or leaving the student unattended. If you believe the student may present a harm to himself or others, take him to the emergency room immediately and make your concerns clearly known to the ER staff.

Chapter 7:
Other Conditions Affecting Adaptation to College

J erry is a first-year student residing on your floor. He asks to speak with you one evening shortly after he received his mid-term grades. Jerry reports he received fairly good marks in high school, but felt he had to work much harder and spend more time studying than his peers. At college, he has found that he cannot keep up with the pace and volume of work.

Jerry has a learning disorder.

Previously described in general as dyslexia, various problems that make studying a challenge now are considered learning disorders. Reading, mathematics and disorders of written expression, alone or in combination, may seriously inhibit academic performance.

Although students these days often come to campus with an existing diagnosis of a learning disorder, some will not have been evaluated prior to entering college. Most campuses now have learning resource centers that can evaluate, monitor and establish individual programs for students with these difficulties, allowing them to succeed academically. If you discover a resident has a previously diagnosed learning disorder or you suspect an underlying issue, reassure them that help is available and help them to identify campus resources that can assist with evaluation and accommodation.

Between 4-5 percent of entering first-year college students present with some form of Attention Deficit/Attention Deficit Hyperactivity Disorder (ADD/ADHD). These students are at risk for lower GPA's, increased incidence of academic probation and more reported academic problems than their peer group. Males generally are more commonly affected than females. Other co-morbid conditions such as depression and substance abuse are frequent.

The decrease in structure at college relative to high school may bring out symptoms. Typical problems include inattention and distractibility, hyperactivity and impulsivity. The provision of structure may help these students with organization. Tutors may be helpful and accommodation, such as additional time for tests, may be indicated.

Most students with ADD/ADHD respond well to medication, which helps with focus and organization. They may need assistance with medication compliance, and it is extremely important to caution these students not to share their prescription medication with other students. There is significant overlap with many students having ADD/ADHD and learning disorders, so a comprehensive professional evaluation is crucial. Finding nonjudgmental ways to promote the kinds of services available to students who have or suspect they may have an issue with attention deficit disorder may increase the likelihood they will seek and comply with treatment.

Students diagnosed with Autistic Spectrum Illnesses and Asperger's Syndrome are also seen more commonly on campus these days. These disorders generally present with problems in social interactions characterized by non-verbal behaviors such as avoiding eye contact or unusual postures. Sensory integration issues – i.e., sensitivity to touch, light, or sound – also can lead to discomfort and difficulties living in community. These students tend to have problems developing peer relations, restricted patterns of interest, and limited ability to empathize with others. These features may be accompanied by specific learning disorders. Medication, counseling and academic assistance are indicated for these students. Moreover, helping other residents to understand, respect and respond with empathy to students who may cause uncomfortable social interactions is an important service you can provide as a resident assistant.

Chapter 8:
Supporting the Emotional Health and Resilience of LGBTQ Students

The past decade has witnessed a number of changes in the treatment of gay, lesbian, bisexual, transgendered or queer individuals. The campaign for marriage equality, anti-bullying efforts like "It Gets Better," Jason Collins emerging as the first openly gay professional athlete, and musings about a potential boycott of the Sochi Olympics due to anti-gay legislation in Russia—are all leading indicators that times are changing, at least for some individuals, and in some communities. For others, attending college may provide an escape from homophobic and hostile communities, schools, or families. The transition, while full of hope and possibility, also may accompany uncertainty of what lies ahead.

While the vast majority of LGBTQ students successfully adapt to life in college and go on to fulfilling careers and healthy relationships, each student is unique and comes to college with his or her own strengths, challenges and personal experiences. And while sexual orientation and gender expression is only one aspect of one person's identity, there are concerns specific to LGBTQ students of which resident assistants should be aware in order to understand and effectively intervene should a student need support or assistance. Indeed, the presence of supportive mentors, gay/straight alliance organizations, inclusive curriculums and comprehensive anti-bullying campaigns all appear to serve as protective factors for mitigating adverse psychological and behavioral effects of victimization. In short, you can make a difference.

Previous school-based trauma

For many students, K-12 education was neither a safe nor rewarding experience. The most recent National School Climate Survey (2011), prepared by the Gay, Lesbian, Straight Education Network, demonstrates ongoing concerns about the hostile environments some LGBTQ students continue to encounter in schools today. Overwhelming majorities of students reported hearing negative remarks about gender expression or sexual orientation, including from teachers and staff – 63.5 percent felt unsafe because of their sexual orientation and 43.9 percent because of their gender expression. Verbal and physical harassment, including cyberbullying, were frequently reported, and almost a fifth of students reported being the victim of physical assault. Moe than 60 percent of students indicate they did not report harassment to staff because they didn't believe action would be taken or that reporting it could make things worse. About a third of students who did report an incident said that school staff did nothing in response.

For students who were consistently bullied or targeted by peers or even staff for mistreatment, distrust and anxiety may permeate their relationship to education. Some may have developed social phobias, and relied upon school avoidance tactics to decrease their visibility at school and minimize opportunities for mistreatment. Avoidance can have many unfortunate side effects. Students experiencing higher levels of victimization were less likely to plan to attend college and reported lower GPAs than their less frequently victimized peers.

Depression, self-esteem, and suicidality

Students who are bullied for their sexual orientation or gender expression are more likely to experience depression, low self-esteem and suicidal thoughts than their peers. A historical dearth of positive role models or supportive adults may also contribute to emotional difficulty, although pop cultural representations of gay individuals and couples have become increasingly common and more positive in recent years. Moreover, efforts like Dan Savage's "It Gets Better" and "The Trevor Project" are shining a light on the experience of LGBTQ youth and providing support and guidance to students in need. However, resident assistants should be aware of these risk factor when concerned about and determining whether or not to intervene with a particular individual.

Internalized homophobia

Internalized homophobia is a phenomenon that also can negatively affect student's emotional well being. All individuals have to examine and confront their own homophobic tendencies or reactions, conscious and unconscious, which are often based on misinformation, cultural stereotypes, or religious messages. For LGBTQ students, such attitudes can lead to feelings of shame, guilt, and anxiety, which can complicate decisions about coming out, exploring relationships, and even connecting openly with others. Be alert to homophobic comments and behaviors, whether overt or covert, and try to engage students in open, supportive discussions about the genesis and impact of such attitudes and work to model appropriate self-acceptance and respect for diversity.

Coming Out

It is important to understand that for many LGBTQ students, coming out is not a singular event but rather an ongoing journey. Some individuals will choose to be out with close friends only. Others may be out on campus, but not at home or with family. Still others may be comfortable coming out to peers, but not to professors or other authority figures. Try not to make any assumptions about where an individual may be along the "out" continuum and don't be alarmed or confused by what may appear to be inconsistency or ambivalence. Be supportive, listen, and follow your resident's lead.

On a related note, the college years are a time of experimentation, as all students work to develop and concretize a sense of personal identity. It is important to note that individuals may experiment with sexual partners or gender expression, and that some amount of fluidity is normal. Some students, particularly transgendered individuals, may not feel comfortable fully identifying as gay, straight, male or female, and while the uncertainty may be unsettling to others (e.g., peers or administrators) intent on neat categorization, patient acceptance for where an individual is and chooses to be needs to take precedence.

Physical health

All students need to learn appropriate self-care during college and have access to supportive, quality medical and physical health services. It is especially important to help LGBTQ students identify providers who will be compassionate and accepting about their individual health concerns. Sexually-transmitted infections are common among all college students, but incidents are higher among gay and lesbian college students, which makes practicing safe sex and accessible treatment important priorities.

Moreover, alcohol, drug and tobacco use tends to be greater among LGBTQ students, and RA's should be alert to any resident that may have difficulty controlling substance use.

Chapter 9:
Eating Disorders and Body Image

J ulie, *a first-year student in your residence, is vocalizing concerns about weight gain. She began to follow a very strict diet as well as an intense exercise program, running eight to ten miles a day before most other residents even were out of bed. Despite an increasing appearance of emaciation, Julie continues to express concern that she is overweight.*

Julie is experiencing an acute episode of anorexia nervosa.

The two major categories of eating disorders are anorexia nervosa and bulimia nervosa. Both involve disordered eating behaviors and altered perceptions of weight and body image. More than 90 percent of persons affected are female. Certain students are at greater risk, such as models, dancers and athletes.

Individuals with anorexia nervosa generally severely restrict their food intake. This may be accompanied by purging or brutal exercise regimes. There is a significant mortality rate associated with cardiac rhythm abnormalities. Anorexia nervosa is a rare disorder, affecting 0.5 percent of the population. Anorectic individuals generally require specialized long-term treatment.

Bulimia nervosa is characterized by episodes of binge eating followed by purging, fasting, or excessive exercise. Patients tend to maintain a normal weight. Binging usually involves sweet, high calorie foods, which are consumed in large quantities over a short period of time, often in secret. Between 1-3 percent of college-age females are typically affected. The disorder is seen with much less frequency in males. The disorder is often chronic, lasting for years and even decades. There is marked dissatisfaction with the body and concern about becoming overweight. Shame causes the affected individual to be very secretive. Referral to a program specializing in eating disorders is indicated.

Disordered eating and issues with body image can affect both males and females without meeting the threshold for a specific eating disorder. For example, research shows that men are more likely to place an emphasis on muscle build and being too thin. It is important as a resident advisor to ensure messages about healthy self-image and health living trump cultural cues and concerns toward beauty, objectification and thinness. A recent *New York Times* article, "Fat Talk Compels, but Carries a Cost," postulates that "fat talk is so embedded among women that it often reflects not how the speaker actually feels about her body but how she is expected to feel about it." Encourage your students to talk about their struggles with body image and model healthy dialogue around the body. Offer healthy but delicious snacks during floor events in order to demonstrate that food can be a fun, energizing reward, rather than a guilty pleasure. And plan activities that honor a healthy life style, like building a community garden or participating in a 5K-charity walk.

Chapter 6:
Substance Abuse

*S*am, *a first-year student on your floor of the residence hall, has been developing a reputation for heavy weekend binge drinking. A reasonable, conscientious student, Sam appears to lose control after the end of classes on Friday. Tonight, his roommate reports that Sam won't wake up and is laying face up in a pool of vomit.*

Sam is suffering from alcohol intoxication, and appears to be struggling with a substance abuse disorder.

The use and misuse of psychoactive substances is rampant on American campuses and appears to be becoming more prevalent. Patterns of substance abuse involve the self-administration of substances with psychoactive properties to alter one's subjective state and experience of their environment under inappropriate circumstances or in amounts greater than generally acceptable. Substances abused include alcohol, illicit drugs and prescription medication.

In terms of sheer numbers, alcohol presents the most significant problems in the college population. Consider the following numbers:

- Among college students during a 12-month period, 6 percent meet diagnostic criteria for alcohol dependence and 31 percent meet criteria for alcohol abuse.
- Half of all college students binge drink and/or abuse prescription or illicit drugs

- A full 80 percent of campus arrests for rape, drunk driving or assault are alcohol-related
- About 1700 students die annually from unintended alcohol-related incidents.

Despite these statistics, substance misuse, particularly of alcohol, is widely accepted as a rite of passage during college, and binge drinking (defined as drinking with the intention of becoming drunk) is more often than not, an accepted norm. So how is one to decipher when substance use has crossed the line to abuse, and that help may be required?

Understanding the diagnostic criteria for substance use disorders can be a helpful place to start. Basically, substance use is classified as substance abuse when the pattern of use has become maladaptive, leading to "clinically significant impairment or distress." In other words, it's subjective, but clear indicators of distress include failure to fulfill work obligations (e.g., skipping class or failing to complete assignments), failing to account for risk while drinking or on drugs (e.g., driving, walking unaccompanied at night while intoxicated), and most importantly, continued use despite persistent interpersonal troubles (e.g., losing friends or significant others due to substance use).

Substance dependence is a more serious disorder characterized by the need for increased amounts of substance to bring about intoxication (e.g., tolerance), withdrawal symptoms (e.g., headaches or nausea, often "treated" with further drinking), and ongoing deterioration of functioning and social connectedness. Understanding the physiological effects of commonly abused substances can provide resident advisors with the information they need to make informed, sensitive interventions.

Alcohol Use
Alcohol intoxication proceeds in stages depending on time and

amount ingested. Early disinhibition produces euphoria and tends to have a calming effect. However, alcohol poisoning is a frequent outcome of binge drinking. Confusion and stupor eventually progress to a comatose state. Depression of the central nervous system slows breathing and suppresses the gag reflect leading to vomiting and potential aspiration of stomach contents into the lungs. Although the individual may have passed out and appears to be "sleeping it off," blood alcohol levels may continue to rise secondary to absorption of alcohol. Slow respirations, irregular breathing, blue tinged lips or hypothermia constitute a medical emergency and necessitate a call to 911.

Marijuana (Cannabis)

Marijuana is the most used illicit drug on campuses across the country. (As of publication, marijuana continues to be illegal in the majority of states) Over a 15-year period beginning in the mid 1990s, use of marijuana among college students doubled. Relief of stress and social acceptance were noted as the most common reasons for use.

The "high" from marijuana produces a sense of well-being, followed by drowsiness, and impairments in perception, coordination, reaction time and attention. Extremely high levels of intoxication may cause paranoia and psychotic symptoms. Physical signs and symptoms of acute intoxication include red eyes, increased appetite, dry mouth and increased heart rate. Symptoms may be exacerbated by mixing cannabis and alcohol.

Operating a motor vehicle while high on cannabis appears to be as dangerous as driving under the influence of alcohol. Chronic daily use of marijuana has been reported to lead to an amotivational syndrome characterized by apathy and loss of interests and goals.

College students who smoke marijuana heavily develop demonstrable neuropsychological deficits including problems with attention, new learning, verbal fluency, poor concentration and weak analytic skills. These deficits persist beyond the time of intoxication. Heavy users of marijuana in college generally seek treatment only after academic, social or physical performance have significantly deteriorated.

Cocaine

Cocaine is an illicit stimulant that is highly abused. During intoxication, individuals experience euphoria, hypersexuality, and hypervigilance. Increased doses over time may lead to a form of delirium, seizures, cardiac problems, and death. Withdrawal following use of cocaine results in a "crash" characterized by fatigue and dysphoria as well as craving for more drug.

Hallucinogenic Drugs

Hallucinogenic drugs have been used on college campuses since the 1960s. LSD, PCP and MDMA (a.k.a., ecstasy) are the most commonly abused. Generally, acute intoxication with these compounds produces perceptual alterations, mood lability, and altered thought processes. Pupils are dilated and heart rate generally increases. Treatment for an acute "bad trip" involves reassurance and a calm setting, and may require several hours to "come down."

Prescription Drugs

Abuse of prescription drugs is up more than 450 percent in the past 15 years and now rivals illicit drugs as a major cause of overdose death. Prescription drugs most frequently misused include narcotic analgesics (e.g., Vicodin, Oxy-Contin), anxiolytic medication (e.g., Xanax and other benzodiazepines) and stimulants (e.g., amphetamines and Ritalin).

These medications are often "shared" by individual with a valid prescription. This is a very dangerous and potentially lethal practice. Acute intoxication with narcotic and anxiolytics generally presents with lethargy, somnolence, poor coordination and confusion.

Despite cultural norms that minimize the dangers of substance misuse, inappropriate use of psychoactive substances is a major health concern on all college campuses throughout the country. It is important to note that no two individuals will respond to substances in exactly the same way. What may be a typical night of consumption for one student may be a lethal amount for another. A student with a family history of alcohol dependency may be less able to tolerate social drinking, and will be at risk to develop his or her own substance abuse problem. Some students will use substances to celebrate special occasions, while others will rely on them for coping with day-to-day disappointments. An alert resident assistant can play a significant role in identifying students with substance abuse issues and help make potentially lifesaving referrals to supportive treatment. This includes becoming familiar with local chapters of Alcoholics Anonymous (AA), Narcotics Anonymous (NA), and Al-Anon, a program to support individuals with a family member suffering from alcoholism.

Chapter 11:
Sexual Assault

*S*arah *was at a house party with a few of her girlfriends and was having a good time getting to know Steve, a guy from her English class. They were drinking and shooting pool when she started to get a little warm in the crowded room. Steve invited her up to his room to get a little air. They talked for awhile longer, but when Sarah wanted to go back downstairs, Steve teased her for leading him on, and demanded oral sex before he allowed her to leave. When Sarah refused, Steve threatened to keep her there, and to spread rumors about her the following day. He held her down and forced her to perform oral sex. When someone interrupted them, Sarah ran out of the room. Embarrassed and ashamed, she grabbed her things and left the party.*

Sarah was the victim of a sexual assault.

Sexual assault is far too common on college campuses today. In fact, college age women are more likely to experience sexual assault than any other age group. Among college age men, statistics show that around 5 percent of males have also experienced some form of sexual assault. Across both genders, experts estimate that assaults tend to go vastly unreported. Like Sarah, most assaults are perpetrated by individuals known to the victim. Another reality is that stalking and cyberstalking are most prevalent among women ages 18-24, a fact that requires specific attention due to the risk it presents on college campuses today.

Sexual assault specifically refers to any unwanted sexual contact that stops short of rape. This would include unwanted touching or fondling. Rape is defined as forced sexual intercourse, which includes vaginal, anal or oral penetration by a body part or an object. Children and adults can be raped, as can gay or straight individuals. Force can include actual physical violence or the threat of violence, and if a victim doesn't give a verbal "No" out of fear of additional harm, it is still considered rape.

It is also important to understand the rules around consent, especially on college campuses where drugs and alcohol so often play a role in sexual activity. In order to provide consent, a victim must be old enough (16 or 18 years old depending on the state); he or she must have the capacity to consent (cannot be disabled, drugged, drunk or unconscious); and he or she must have agreed to the sexual conduct (which means that if a person withdraws consent during a sexual act, the person must stop).

We share these definitions, not to assist RA's in litigating resident claims of sexual assault, but in effort to combat some cultural norms that contribute to the climate in which sexual assault continues to occur. Unfortunately, the majority of sexual assaults occur when college women are alone with a man they know, at night, in the privacy of a residence. Risk factors include living on campus, being unmarried, drinking frequently, and prior victimization. While some will claim such realities unfairly blame the victim, it behooves entire communities to understand the risks involved in college life, and to take steps to protect ones friends and oneself from harm. This means both men and women can play a role in protecting one another by actively avoiding potentially ambivalent situations that leave both partners embarrassed, ashamed or unsure of what occurred.

Rape and sexual assault have both short- and long-term consequences for victims, loved ones, and communities. Often, survivors experience disruptions physically, emotionally, cognitively and interpersonally, and tend to suffer symptoms long after the attack itself. Survivors of sexual assault are at higher risks for depression, PTSD, anxiety, drug and alcohol abuse, and relationship difficulties. These risks indicate the importance of early and sustained intervention in assisting individuals through the immediate aftermath of assault and into recovery. Even in cases where consent was ambivalent and prosecution unlikely, shame, self-doubt, and guilt can still be prevalent and deserves support.

If someone you know is sexually assaulted, the most important thing to do is ensure the environment is safe and the person no longer feels threatened. The assault should be reported to campus authorities as well as to the police by calling 911. Assist the victim in writing down the details of the attack and preserve any physical evidence—the survivor should not shower, change clothes, brush teeth, etc. If the person must change, he or she should keep the clothes in a plastic bag. Insist on medical attention. There can be injuries that go unnoticed in the immediate aftermath, and it is important to discuss the risks of STIs and pregnancy. If the victim suspects she was drugged, request a urine sample be collected at the hospital, and that they conduct a rape kit to collect forensic evidence. Again, individuals can always change their mind about pressing charges in the future, but such steps will ensure they have the option available to them. If individuals need advice, counseling, or other forms of support, recommend that they call the National Sexual Assault Hotline, 1.800.656.HOPE. Provide referrals to community support, and help the individual identify trusted friends and family with whom you can coordinate ongoing support.

Perhaps it is more likely for you to be approached, after the fact, by a resident who is recovering from a sexual assault. There are a number of things you can do to provide a safe and nonjudgmental atmosphere that will help support him or her through their ongoing attempts to cope. First and foremost, BELIEVE the individual. For many survivors, shame, guilt and self-

Table 3: RAINN's Back-To-School Tips

Trust your instincts. If you feel unsafe in any situation, go with your gut. If you see something suspicious, contact your resident assistant or campus police immediately.

Avoid being alone or isolated with someone you don't know well. Let a trusted friend know where you are and who you are with.

Get to know your surroundings and learn a well-lit route back to your dorm or residence. If you are new to the campus, familiarize yourself with the campus map and know where the emergency phones are.

Be careful when leaving online away messages. Leaving information about your whereabouts or activities reveals details of your location that are accessible to everyone. Avoid putting your dorm room, campus address, or phone number on your personal profile where everyone can see it.

Form a buddy system when you go out. Arrive with your friends, check in with each other throughout the night, and leave together. Don't go off alone. Make a secret signal with your friends for when they should intervene if you're in an uncomfortable situation.

Never loan your room key to anyone and always lock your door. Don't let strangers into your room.

Practice safe drinking. Don't accept drinks from people you don't know or trust and never leave your drink unattended – if you've left your drink alone, just get a new one. Always watch your drink being prepared. At parties, don't drink from punch bowls or other large, common open containers.

Watch out for your friends. If a friend seems out of it, is way too intoxicated for the amount of alcohol they've had, or is acting out of character, get him or her to a safety place immediately. If you suspect that you or a friend has been drugged, call 911, and be explicit with doctors about your symptoms.

Don't let your guard down. The college campus environment can foster a false sense of security. Don't assume people you've just met will look out for your best interests; remember that they are essentially strangers.

Try not to go out alone at night. Walk with roommates or someone you trust. If you'll be walking home alone, ask a trusted friend to accompany you. Avoid the ATM and jogging at night. Don't put music headphones in both ears so you can be more aware of your surroundings.

doubt around their own responsibility for the attack keeps them from seeking the support they need and deserve. It is never the victim's fault that they were assaulted, and ensuring that your posture communicates this conviction is important for creating a safe atmosphere and in combating cultural norms that reinforce such beliefs. Secondly, allow the survivor to take the lead. They may seek advice from you about finding support, reporting the assault, pressing charges, or receiving medical attention. While you should be armed with accurate information and community resources, remember that it is up to the individual to make their own choices. You can support and empower them to make pro-active decisions, but try not to exert your control, no matter how badly you want to help. Finally, relax and be ready to listen. You don't have to know the perfect thing to say, but you can be a safe and supportive presence as the person begins to explore their own feelings about what occurred and the aftermath of what it means.

According to RAINN (Rape, Abuse and Incest National Net-work), the following are some common sense practices that can help keep college students safe. Consider sharing these with your residents, male and female, to raise awareness about the realities of sexual assault, and the responsibilities we all share in reducing risk.

Chapter 12:
Suicide,
Self-destructive and
Violent Behavior

Louise, a first-year student in your residence hall, appears to have changed since the beginning of the school year. Rather than her usual outgoing and energetic self, she seems withdrawn and isolative. Louise appears somewhat haggard, has lost a noticeable amount of weight, and has started to miss some early morning classes. When asked directly if she was ok or if she had thoughts of harming herself, she became tearful and acknowledged she had been thinking a lot about how much easier things would be for everyone if she were gone.

Louise is experiencing suicidal ideation.

Suicide is the second leading cause of death in the college-age population (after accidents) and is a highly preventable cause of death. The great majority of college-age suicide attempters are suffering from an acute psychiatric illness, typically a mood disorder. It is important to note that these illnesses are very responsive to treatment. Women tend to make suicide attempts four times more often than men, however, men are three times more likely to succeed. This is generally due to difference in the lethality of the attempts (medication overdose vs. guns, respectively).

Identification of a potentially suicidal individual is a critical first step in avoiding a potentially lethal act and initiating treatment. Depression, hopelessness, giving away possessions, talking about suicide, and securing the means to kill oneself (e.g., hording pills, buying a gun) are all indications that a person may be considering suicide. If you have concerns, it is critical to *directly inquire* about suicidal ideation, for example with questions like: "Have you been thinking about dying?"; "Do you think things would be better if you weren't around?"; "Have you been thinking about harming yourself?"; and "Have you been considering suicide?"

There is an old and untrue myth that mentioning suicide may trigger an attempt. In fact, broaching the subject often is ameliorative to an individual with suicidal thoughts, and direct, open questions are the most helpful. Try to avoid closing down the conversation before it begins with questions like, "You're not thinking about suicide, are you?" This could be shaming to the individual; if he or she feels the thoughts are wrong or abhorrent to you, it is likely they will conceal them in order to save face.

It is important to listen attentively and non-judgmentally to the individual. Encourage them to express their feelings and respond with comfort and concern. Try to remember that when desperate, suicide is viewed as a solution to a problem. So help the individual to define what problem it is they are attempting to solve, empathize with the difficulty they are facing, and attempt to discuss alternative solutions. Let them know that suicide is never their only choice.

In terms of assessing the seriousness of suicidal thinking, there are a number of questions that are helpful. Have they considered a method or do they have a plan? Do they have the means to carry out their plan? Have they set a date or time? How potentially lethal is the plan? The answers to these questions will also alert you to the level of immediate threat, and what kind of referral or intervention is necessary (e.g., referral to the counseling center or immediate hospitalization).

Thinking openly and conveying an accepting attitude is very important. Avoid any request to keep your discussion secret. Make it clear that the situation requires an immediate and sufficient response and that the person's health and well-being are important to you. The individual should not be left alone while arrangements are being made for an urgent evaluation at student health or the emergency room. The individual should be escorted to the site of the evaluation, underscoring both the seriousness of the situation and the response.

Self Harm

Some individuals who are not actively suicidal engage in self-injurious behaviors. Many of these individuals cut themselves when feeling stressed or emotionally overwhelmed. They often report a relief of tension or a reduction in anger toward themselves as a result of the cutting. Wrists, arms, thighs and legs are most often cut, and females are three times more likely to engage in self-injurious behavior than males. Intoxication with alcohol or other substances often lowers the threshold for cutting. Individuals who cut generally will engage in this behavior chronically, and often require intensive therapy.

For many individuals, cutting or other self-harming behavior is intensely private and can have an addictive quality. If you suspect a resident is engaging in self-harming behavior, it is important to inquire about it non-judgmentally and try to remember that the person is causing himself or herself pain in an attempt to soothe emotional turmoil. Cutting often can indicate a history of sexual or physical trauma, and individuals exhibiting self-injurious behavior should be referred to a qualified therapist for ongoing monitoring and support.

Suicidality and self-harm are difficult subjects. Even professionals are often personally affected by working with individuals suffering from this depth of emotional pain and desperation. If you find yourself in a situation where you are helping a resident deal with suicidal ideation, remember to seek help and support from your colleagues and mentors. Always protect resident confidentiality, but don't be ashamed if these kinds of situations cause you to want to talk about your own fears and concerns. To care for and be available to others, you need to take care of yourself.

Violent Behavior

In recent years, news headlines have featured articles about campus violence, at times with dramatic loss of life. From the "Texas Tower" in Austin in 1966 to more recent events at Virginia Tech, these occurrences have become legendary.

It is important to realize that these kinds of violent actions are extraordinarily rare. The potential perpetrators of such acts will tend to be "loners," very isolative and often preoccupied by unusual political or cultural views. There is a significant tendency to distrust others and to maintain a paranoid stance. Concerns about such individuals should be shared with your student services supervisors before a situation can escalate to violence.

Appendix: Resources

Local Resources
Often the most useful referral resources are available in your local area. Your administration can provide you with information on local crisis lines and outreach, emergency rooms, approved local mental health providers, etc.

National Resources
General Mental Health Concerns:
National Alliance for the Mentally Ill

Depression and Bipolar Support Alliance: www.dbsalliance.org

Substance Abuse:
AA, NA and Ala-Anon

Almost Alcoholic: Is My (Or My Loved One's Drinking) a Problem? (2012). Joseph Nowinski PhD and M.D. Robert Doyle MD

Sexual Assault:
RAINN: Rape Abuse and Incest National Network, www.rainn.org

National Sexual Assault Hotline 1.800.656.HOPE(4673) |

LGBTQ/Ally:
Athlete Ally: www.athleteally.org

Parents, Families and Friends of Lesbians and Gays (PFLAG): www.pflag.org

It Gets Better Project: www.itgetsbetter.org

The Trevor Project 1-866-4-U-TREVOR (866-488-7386)
The Trevor Project is the leading national organization providing crisis intervention and suicide prevention services to lesbian, gay, bisexual, transgender, and questioning youth.

The GLBT National Help Center: www.glnh.org
Hotline: 1-888-THE-GLNH (888-843-4564)

Youth Talkline: 1-800-246-PRIDE (800-246-7743) or Online peer chat: http://www.glnh.org/chat/index.html

Suicide Prevention:
Suicide hotline – 1-800-SUICIDE

About the Authors

A passion for higher education and mental health advocacy, as well as an ongoing commitment to ensuring the success of their shared alma mater – Ripon College in Ripon, Wis. – connects the authors. Three graduates across four decades bring together a rich and multifaceted approach to connecting with and educating college students and staff.

Philip K. McCullough, MD has been involved in college student health service since 1971. A member of the faculty at the Feinberg School of Medicine of Northwestern University since 1976, he is a board certified psychiatrist and a Distinguished Life Fellow of the American Psychiatric Association. He has worked in private practice, community mental health, and inpatient psychiatric facilities for more than 40 years. A committed educator, he is also the recipient of numerous teaching awards from Northwestern University Medical School, where he is a member of the faculty. He has served on the Ripon College Board of Trustees since 1996.

Kristen M. Granchalek, LCSW is cofounder of Alliance | Collaborative Psychotherapy, a private therapy practice that specializes in treating young adults in transition. Before pursuing psychotherapy training, Kristen spent more than a decade as a higher education consultant and has presented nationally and internationally on issues of strategic concern in post-secondary education. She served on the Ripon College Alumni Board from 2006-12 and continues to mentor current students and recent graduates on professional development. Kristen maintains an active market research practice that focuses on college and graduate-level students, their needs and priorities.

Chris Ogle, MA is Vice President and Dean of Students at Ripon College. A 30-year veteran of higher education administration, Chris has served as Hall Director and Director of Resident Life at Ripon College. Chris received his Master's Degree in Higher Education/Counseling from the University of Wisconsin-Oshkosh.

www.ingramcontent.com/pod-product-compliance
Lightning Source LLC
Chambersburg PA
CBHW050603280326
41933CB00011B/1961